T0193588

The Life of Joseph

LEONA SMITH

All Scriptures are taken from King James Version of the Bible

WestBow Press books may be ordered through booksellers or by contacting:

WestBow Press
A Division of Thomas Nelson & Zondervan
1663 Liberty Drive
Bloomington, IN 47403
www.westbowpress.com
1 (866) 928-1240

ISBN: 978-1-5127-9416-8 (sc)
ISBN: 978-1-5127-9417-5 (e)

Library of Congress Control Number: 2017910393

Print information available on the last page.

WestBow Press rev. date: 09/11/2017

WESTBOW
P R E S S®
A DIVISION OF THOMAS NELSON
& ZONDERVAN

This book is dedicated to all God's people in the world, big and small. It's an action packed story, from the beginning to the end. It can be Enjoyed, by a wide range of ages. Adults will really enjoy, reading this Story to children. They'll love the drawings that bring to life, this true Bible story. Children will naturally love it, with all of its characters.

I took special care, in keeping the story, as explained in the bible, by telling the story in a way, that children can understand it, more fully. I was inspired to create these, life like pictures, of the characters, in the story of Joseph. I wanted their to be as many pictures as possible, to keep the attention of a child, and also, make the story come alive, for them. The pictures describe the action, love, joy and sorrows of this marvelous story of Joseph and his family. It tells how God came lovingly through, for not only Joseph and his family, in the time of a famine, but also how, the whole world was then saved, from starvation, by God's wisdom, given to Joseph.

Joseph endured, in times of great stress, trials, sorrow, rejection, and disappointments. When all the world, was to have, a deadly famine, the Lord showed Joseph a way, to save people, all over the world, by saving a little, each day.

Joseph's family, did make mistakes, that was not good, but God caused all things to work together for their good, and the worlds good also. Though all was not good, that happened to Joseph's family, yet, God had a great plan, in bringing them, out of their circumstances.

Leona Smith

"The Son's of Jacob"

To Jacob was born 12 son's in all,
And these were their names.
    From the oldest to the youngest,
This is how they came.

The 1st was Rueben
  The 2nd was Simeon
    The 3rd was Levi
      The 4th was Judah
        The 5th was Dan
          The 6th was Naphtali
          The 7th was Gad
            The 8th was Asher
              The 9th was Issachar
              The 10th was Zebulon
            The 11th was Joseph
And years later, The 12th ^{son,,} was Benjamin

But, Benjamin's mother Rachel, died at Benjamin's birth.
    And a daughter was born to Jacob, named Dinah,
And just before Joseph's birth. And one unnamed daughter, Jacob had.
    Which was born later, and was the 33rd descendant of, Jacob's wife, Leah.

Joseph was the son of Jacob
And Jacob was the son of Isaac;
Isaac was the son of Abraham,
To whom God made promises to, in Canaan Land.

Now Jacob, whom God named Israel,
Lived with his twelve sons, and family in Canaan land;
Joseph being seventeen years old, at the time,
Was feeding the flock with his brother's, at the time.

Joseph heard an evil report
That his brothers did say;
Joseph told his father their evil report
When he got back home, that day.

Now Israel loved Joseph more than,
All his other children;
Because while Jacob, now being in his old age,
Had Joseph much closer to him.

Jacob, who was named Israel, by the Lord God,
Did make Joseph a coat of many colors;
The brothers, saw that their father loved Joseph,
More than all the others.

After that, they all hated him,
And could not speak to him, peaceably again;
Joseph dreamed a dream, and told it to them;
And they hated him more, after he had told it, to them.
                    Gen. 37: 1-5

Joseph again the second time had a dream,
And said unto his brothers;
    "Hear, I pray you this dream,
    Which I have dreamed."

"For we were binding our sheaves in the field
And lo, my sheave arose, and stood upright;"
"But, your sheaves stood all around mine,
And bowed down in obeisance to mine."

His brothers said to Joseph,
"Will you honestly have power over us to dominate"?
    And they hated him more for his dreams,
And for the words, that he did say.

And he dreamed yet another dream,
And told it to his brothers, again;
    Joseph said, "Behold the sun, moon, and eleven stars,
Bowed down in obedience to me, again."

And he told it to his father,
    And his father rebuked him, saying, too!
'Shall your mother, I and your brothers,
    Come to bow ourselves down, on the earth to you?"

His brothers envied him.
    But his father thought about his sayings;
Israel his father, listened in wonder,
    To what his son was saying.
            Gen. 37: 6-11

The brothers of Joseph went to feed,
 Their fathers flock, in Shechem;
Israel said to Joseph,
 "I will, send you there to them."

 Israel said, "Go and see if all is well,
With the flocks and your brother's"
 So he sent Joseph out of the valley of Hebron,
And then he came to Shechem.

 A man found Joseph wandering in a field, and Joseph said,
"Can you tell me where my brother's flocks are being feed?
 He said," I heard them say let us go to Dotham!"
So Joseph found them there as the man said, in Dothan.

 When they saw Joseph afar off, before he was near,
They said, "Look the dreamer cometh there!"
 They said, "Come now and let us slay him, here."
"And let us cast him into a pit somewhere!"

 But Rueben heard it, and took him out of their hands.
Rueben said," Let us not kill him!"
 "Shed no blood, but cast him into a pit, in the wilderness."
"And lay no hand on him!"

 But Rueben had said this,
To take Joseph out of their hands;
 For later, he would take him to his father.
That is what, he had planned.
     Gen. 37: 12-22

"The Midianites and Ishmaelites"

When Joseph came near to his brothers,
They stripped off him, his coat of many colors;
   They took Joseph and threw him into an empty pit,
Which, had no water in it.

   As they sat down to eat bread,
They saw a company coming from Gilead;
   They were Ishmaelites, into Egypt going,
With spices balm and myrrh, to Egypt carrying.

   Then Judah said, "What profit is it for us to slay him,
And hide the blood of our brother here?"
   "For he is our flesh brother, let not our hand be on him!"
"Come let us sell him to the Ishmaelites, going over there!"

   Then there passed by Midianite, merchantmen.
It was they who drew and lifted Joseph out of the pit;
   The Midianites later sold Joseph to the Ishmaelites,
For twenty pieces of silver, and brought him to Egypt.

   When Rueben returned to the pit, for Joseph,
Rueben tore his own clothes, for Joseph was not there;
   Rueben returned to his brothers and said.
"The child is not there, and where can I go, where"?
Gen. 37: 23-30

Joseph's brothers, took Joseph's lovely coat,
That his father had made him, to do something to it;
    They killed one of the young kid goats,
And dipped the coat, into the blood of it.

    They sent the coat of many colors, to their father,
With some of the brother's, it was brought;
    They said to their father, "This we have found"
    "Do you know now, if it's your sons coat or not?"

    Israel knew that it was Joseph's coat, and said,
"It is my son's coat that you've got!"
    "An evil beast hath devoured him!"
"Joseph is without doubt, torn in pieces a lot!"

    Then Israel, the father of Joseph,
Tore his own clothes, that day;
    He put on himself, sackcloth for clothing,
And mourned for his son, many days.

    Then all his daughter's and son's rose up to comfort him.,
But he refused to be comforted by them;
    Israel said, "I'll go down to my grave mourning."
So Joseph's father cried, even more for him.
                Gen. 37: 31-35

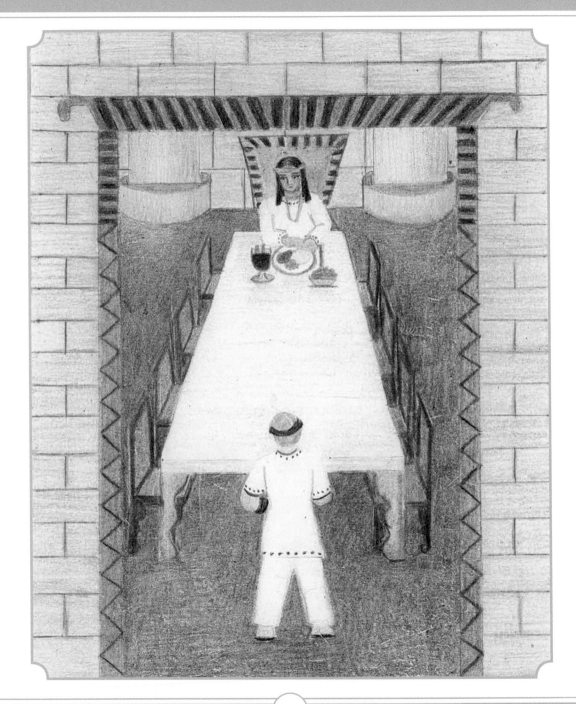

Potiphar was an Egyptian, captain of the guard,
For the king of Egypt's Pharoah;
Potiphar bought Joseph, from some Ishmaelites,
Who brought Joseph to Egypt, you know.

The Lord was with Joseph,
And Joseph was a prosperous man;
Joseph lived in the house of his master,
Named Potiphar, the Egyptian.

His master Potiphar, saw that the Lord,
Was with Joseph, this young man;
The lord made all that Joseph did,
To prosper, in his hand.

Joseph found grace in Pharoah's sight,
And Joseph did, as a servant, and served him;
Potiphar put everything in his own house, in Joseph's hand,
And made Joseph an overseer, for him.

Joseph worked hard, and God blessed Joseph,
And Potiphar's house too, for Josephs sake;
Potiphar left all he owed, in the trust of Joseph,
For he was a goodly and favored person, and not a fake.

The blessing of the Lord was upon all, Potiphar had,
In the house and in the field, too;
Potiphar didn't know what all he did have,
Except for the bread, he did eat, he knew.

Gen. 37: 36-39, 39: 1-6

Time went by and Potiphar's wife, began,
Daily, asking for Joseph to do
something bad;
Joseph always said, "no, for your
husband does trust me,
And how could I make him sad?"

Joseph told her, "There is no one greater,
In this house, than I."
Potiphar has not kept anything from me,
except you.
For you are his wife, that's why!"

"How can I do this wickedness?
And sin against my God?"
She spoke to Joseph, day by day,
But he would not be with her, anyway.

One day, Joseph went into the house.
He was doing his business, as always;
There was none of the men, of the house,
Inside the house, that day.

Potiphar's wife caught Joseph, by his
garment,
Saying the same thing to him, as she
always did;
Joseph left his own garment that she
had grabbed, in her hand.
He ran out of there, yes he did, he ran!

When she saw he left his garment in her
hand, and ran.
She called for the men of the house, saying,
"I cried with a loud voice,
For Joseph came unto me, to do a wrong
thing."

She said, "When he heard, that I lifted
up my voice,
And cried out loud,
Then he left his garment with me."
"He fled and got out!"

Potiphar's wife placed the garment, next
to her,
Until her husband, lord Potiphar came
home, that day;
She said to Potiphar, "The Hebrew
servant,
Which you brought to us, has come in to
mock me, today!"

Gen. 39: 7-14

So Potiphar's wife, told her husband the same words.
And when Joseph's master Potiphar, heard the words,
    He believed her, and was angry.
Potiphar put Joseph into the prison ward.

    Potiphar, was the captain of the guard, over the prison,
In his own house, for Pharoah, in the dungeon;
    Potiphar put Joseph in the prison there, for something he did not do.
But the Lord was with Joseph, there in prison, too.

    The Lord made Joseph prosper, showing him favor and mercy,
With all of the prisoners, too;
    Joseph was made in charge, over all the prisoners,
And all that the prisoners, could do.

    Pharoah became angry with his butler and baker,
Which were his chief officers, the two;
    Pharoah put them in the prison there,
Where, Joseph was in charge of them, and what they could do.

    Both the butler and the baker dreamed a dream one night,
With no way to interpret them, and so they were sad;
    Joseph said, "The meaning belongs to God, and he know."
"Tell me the dreams, that, you two had".

    The butler's dream, Joseph said, "Means Pharoah,
Will bring you back to your work, in three days;
    But, the bakers, dream, means that Pharoah,
Will have you killed, and it happened just that way"
                Gen. 39: 15-23, 40: 1-15

So Pharoah hanged the chief baker,
As Joseph had interpreted to them.
But the chief butler, did not remember Joseph,
But forgot him.

So Joseph had been forgotten, by the chief butler that said,
That he would speak to Pharoah for him;
But he forgot, until two years later, when Pharoah had three dreams
And none of Pharoah's, wise men, could interpret them.

It was then that the butler told Pharoah, saying,
"A Hebrew prison servant, interpreted dreams for two of us."
"This Joseph said, "In three days, I'd go back to work,
But the baker would be killed, and so it was."

So Pharoah sent someone, to call for Joseph,
And to come quickly, out of the dungeons prison;
Joseph shaved and changed his clothes,
And came to stand before him.

Joseph stood before Pharoah, at the age of thirty.
Thirteen years, after being sold;
Pharoah said, "So you can understand,
And interpret dreams, I've heard it told".

Joseph answered Pharoah saying,
It is not me;
But God will give Pharoah,
An answer of peace.

Gen. 39: 22-49

Joseph listened, as Pharoah told him his dreams.
Joseph said, "God has showed you want he is about to do,"
"It is not for me to say, but God will give you,
An answer of peace, which I will this day, tell you."

"There will be seven years of plenty extra good corn,
And fattened healthy cows and food;"
And afterward, they'll be seven years of famine,
With empty ears of corn, skinny cows, and little food."

Joseph said, "Let Pharoah find a wise man in Egypt,
To gather one fifth of the lands food, for seven years,
And keep the corn, under the hand of Pharoah,
So the people won't die, during seven bad famine years."

This was good in the eyes of Pharoah, and his servants.
Pharoah said, "Who can find any one like Joseph, in whom Gods spirit is.
There is no one as wise as wise as you Joseph!
For God has showed you all of this."

Pharoah said, "You will be over my house.
And by your words, you will rule, all the people of Egypt, too.
I've set you over all the lands of Egypt,
And only in the throne, will I be greater than, you!"

Pharoah took of his own ring from his hand,
And put it on Joseph's hand;
Pharoah, put a gold chain, around Joseph's neck,
And arrayed him in vestures of fine linen.

Pharoah made Joseph ride in his own second chariot,
And the servants cried before the people, "Bow the knee"!
Pharoah said to Joseph, "I am Pharoah!"
"And without you, no one shall lift up his own hand or foot, you see."

Pharoah gave Ashnath, a daughter of a priest to Pharoah,
To be his wife, in Egypt's land;
    Ashnath had two sons for Joseph,
Before the seven years of famine began.

    Joseph went out away from Pharoah,
And throughout all the land of Egypt, he did go;
    In the seven plenteous years, the earth brought forth much.
He gathered up all the food needed for seven years, enough.

    Joseph stored up the food of the fields,
In every city around;
    Joseph stored up the food of the fields,
Till he could no longer count.

    Joseph's first son he named Manasseh, for God said,
"The child would make him forget his father's house, and hard work;
    The second son he named Ephriam, for Joseph said,
"God has made me prosper, in the land of my pain and hurt."

    Then the years of good and plenty ended in Egypt,
And all other lands;
    And now the seven years of drought and famines,
As Joseph said, began.

    The drought was in every land,
But in all of Egypt, there was food and bread;
    When all Egypt's food was gone,
The people cried to Pharoah, for bread.

    Pharoah said to all the Egyptians,
"Go to Joseph, and see what he says to you!"
    The famine was bad in Egypt, and all over the earth,
So Joseph opened all the storehouses in Egypt, too.

All countries came to Egypt, before Joseph, to buy corn.
For the famine was bad in all places;
   When Jacob seen that in Egypt there was corn,
He said, "Why do you look at each other's faces?"

   I have heard that there is corn in Egypt!
Israel said to his sons, "Get yourselves down there,
   I've seen and heard, there is corn there to buy."
"Go buy some for us, so that we live and, don't die."

   Joseph's brothers went to Egypt, to buy corn, ten of them.
Now, Israel did not send Benjamin, lest some mischief fall on him;
   The sons of Israel, came among many people that came.
For the famine in Canaan land, was just the same.

   Now Joseph was the governor, over all of Egypt's land.
It was Joseph who sold corn, to all people in all lands;
   Joseph's brother's came before Joseph, the lord and governor of Egypt.
They all bowed down, with their faces to the ground.

   When Joseph saw his brothers, he did know them.
But he behaved himself as a stranger, unto them;
   Joseph spoke roughly, asking them where they were from.
They said, "From Canaan land, is where we are from."

   Joseph said,' You've come to see the bare land, you are spies!"
They said, "We are not spies, but your servants are come, for corn to buy."
   We are all one man's sons, we're true men, and not spies!
But Joseph said, "No, it is as I said, you are spies!

   They said, "Your servants are twelve brothers, of one man."
The sons of one man, living in Canaan land.
   One of father's sons, is gone, and the youngest is with our father, this day.
Joseph said, "You'll prove to me you are not spies, by what you say."

Joseph knew his brothers, but they did not know him.
Joseph remembered the dreams he had, back then.
   The dreams that meant, they'd bow down to him.
He remembered them hating him, for they thought, he wanted to rule them.

   Joseph said, "By the life of Pharoah, you shall be kept in prison."
You shall not leave except, your youngest brother comes here!"
   Send one of you to bring him, to prove your words aren't lies!"
"I'll see if there's truth in you, or else your spies."

   For three days, Joseph put all of them in prison ward.
On the third day, Joseph said, "Do this and live for I fear God."
   "If you are true men, leave one of the brothers in prison to stay,"
While the others carry corn home, for the famine, in their houses, today.

   Joseph said, "Bring your youngest brother to me, to verify,
The words you speak, then you won't die."
   Then they began to say, to each other,
We are guilty of how we treated Joseph, our brother

   They said, "We saw the hurt in him, and his soul in fear,
As he begged us for mercy, and we would not hear."
   They said, "This is why this distress, is come upon us."
Then Rueben said, "Now, his blood is required of us.

   Rueben said, "Didn't I say to you, not to sin against the child,
But you would not hear?"
   They didn't know that Joseph could understand them.
For, he was speaking to them, by an interpreter, standing near.

Joseph turned himself away to cry,
And then turned back again to them, to talk to them.
Joseph then took Simeon, away from them,
And bound him before their eyes, in front of them.

So Joseph said, he would hold Simeon in prison,
But all the others, must return to Canaan land.
So, to prove their words were not lies, and not die,
They'd have to bring Benjamin to Egypt's land.

Then Joseph commanded his servants,
To fill their sacks with corn and food, for the way.
Joseph said, "Put each man's money, they've paid for corn,
Back in their sacks," And his servant's did so, right away.

This did Joseph do unto them, before they went.
Then the men put their sacks on their donkeys, and went.
As one opened his sack at the inn, to feed his donkey,
He saw in the pocket of his sack, the bundle of money.

He said to his brothers, "My money, it is back in my sack!"
Then their hearts failed them, for fear.
They said one to another,
"What is this that God is doing to us, here?"

When Jacob's sons, came to him in
Canaan land,
They told him all that had happened to them.
They said, "The man that is the lord of
the land,
Spoke to us roughly, thinking we were spies
in the land."

We told him, "We are true men, and not
spies."
"We are twelve sons of, one man, but one is
gone, no lie!"
The youngest one, our brother,
Is home in Canaan land, with our father.

"The lord of the country, said unto us,
"Here is how I will know if you are true
men, and not spies."
"Leave one of your brother's, here with
me and go home."
"Be gone and take food for the famine, in
your homes."

Joseph said, "Bring your youngest
brother to me,
And I will know, you are not spies, but
true men."
"Then I'll give you back your brother,
And you'll be able to come and do business,
in the land."

After this, as the others emptied their
sacks,
They and their father saw, the bundles of
money, right back.
Because of the bundles of money, they
were so afraid.
For it was with this same amount of money,
for corn they had paid.

Jacob their father said to them, "Joseph
and Simeon are gone,
And you have taken my children from me."
"And now you will take Benjamin,
All these things are against me."

Rueben, spoke to his father saying, "Give
Benjamin your son to me,
And I'll bring him back to you."
"You may slay my two sons,
If I don't bring him back to you!"

Jacob said, "My son shall not, go down
with you!"
"For his brother and mother are gone, and
he is left alone."
"If mischief happens to him, where
you go,
Then you'll bring down my gray hairs to the
grave, with sorrow."

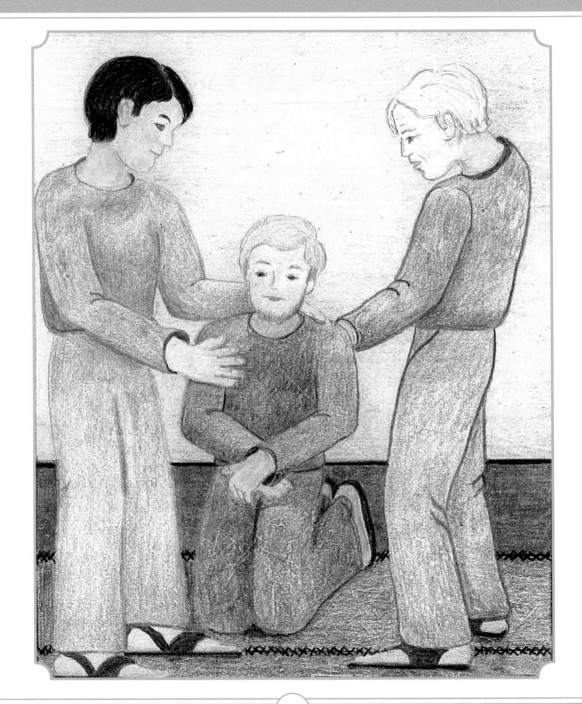

Now the famine, was very bad in the land.
So, when they had eaten, all the corn they'd gotten,
    Israel, their father said unto them.
"Go buy us a little food, again."

    Judah spoke to his father saying, "The man did solemnly say,
If your brother is not with you, you will not see my face."
    Judah said, "If you will send our brother with us, we will go!"
"For the man did say, send your brother, or we cannot see him!"

    So, Israel said, "Why have you treated me so, ill?
By telling this man, that you have another brother?"
    They said, "The man did straightly ask about our family,
If our father was alive, and do you have another brother?"

    Judah said to Israel, "We answered him by what he asked."
"To bring our brother down, did we know, that's what he'd ask?"
    Judah said, "We'll get up and go, if you send the lad with me,
So that we live and don't die, all of the little ones, you and I."

    Judah said, "I will be responsible for him, and if I don't bring him,
Back to you again, I will be the blame forever for him."
    Surely we would have already, returned the second time.
Israel said, "If it must be so now, do this, this time."

    Take the man a present, a little honey, balm, spices,
And myrrh, nuts and almonds."
    Take the best fruit of the land, in your vessels,
And carry it down to the man.

    Israel said, "Take the money in your sacks, and carry it back again.
And take double money to the man, in your hand."
    "Maybe it was a mistake, and take also your brother Benjamin,
And rise up, and go to the man."

The men took Israel's present, with Benjamin,
And double, in their hands, into Egypt's land;
They came and stood, before Joseph having Benjamin.
Then Joseph saw his brother Benjamin, with them.

Joseph having seen Benjamin said, to the ruler of his house,
"Slay kill and make ready, a dinner at my house;
Bring these men to my home, they shall dine with me, at noon.
The man took them to Joseph's house, for Joseph would be home, soon.

Then the men were afraid, because they were at, Josephs home.
They said, "It is because of the money in our sacks, that we're come;
He brought us here, maybe to find some wrong, in us.
Or maybe, take us for slaves, with our donkeys, or to fall on us!

They spoke to the steward at the door, of Joseph's house, there.
They said, "We came the first time and bought food, from here."
"But on the way home at the inn,"
"Everyman's money was back, in everyman's sack, again."

"This money's, of full weight, we've brought it back, in our hands,"
And then the steward brought to them, Simeon back;
He gave them and their donkeys, water to drink,
And brought them into Joseph's house, and washed their feet.

The sons of Israel, prepared Joseph's present, for noon.
They heard, they would eat bread in Joseph's house, soon;
    Joseph came home, and they brought into the house, they're present.
They bowed down to Joseph, and then gave him their present.

    Joseph asked them, "Are you ok, and is your father well?"
"The old man, of who you spoke, is he alive?"
    Our father, your servant is alive, and in good health.
And they bowed down their heads, and bowed again, as well.

    Lifting his eyes, Joseph hurried to leave his brothers.
For his heart yearned to show his love, for his brother;
    Joseph looked for a place to cry, somewhere.
So he entered his chamber, and wept there.

    Joseph washed his face to keep from showing, what he felt.
Joseph then went out and said, "Set on the bread," to his help.
    To eat by themselves, a place was set, for the Egyptians.
For to eat with the Hebrews, was an abomination, to them.

    They sat his brothers before him, the firstborn, Rueben,
And all by their birthright, to the youngest, according to his youth;
    They marveled one to another, having been seated, by age.
Then Joseph took and sent food, unto them, that day.

    Benjamin's food, was five times as much, as theirs.
They drank and were merry, with Joseph there;
    Joseph, in seating them this way, was giving a clue to them,
But still they, did not know him.

Joseph commanded, the steward of his house, saying,
"Fill the men's sacks with food, as much as they can carry;"
Joseph said, "Put every man's money, in his own sacks, pocket,
And put my silver cup and corn money, in the youngest ones, pocket.

The steward did as Joseph had spoken to him.
When the morning was light, for the men.
They were sent away, with their donkeys, all of them.
Now when, they were out of the city, and not too far, from them.

Joseph said to his steward, "Up follow after the men,
And when you catch up to them, say to them."
"Why have you rewarded evil for good, what have you done?"
"Isn't this which, my lord drinks and divines from?"

The steward caught up to them, and spoke these words.
They said, "Why does my lord speak these words?"
"God forbid, that thy servants, should do such a thing."
"The money that we found, in our sacks, we did bring, again"

"How then should we steal, out of my lord's house, gold and silver?"
They said, "With the servant it is found with, let him die, whosoever!"
"We will be, my lord's bondmen." Then the steward said,
"With whom it is found, he shall be my servant, as you said."

"All others will be blameless, the guilty will be with who, the cup is found."
Then they speedily took down each man's sack to the ground;
The steward searched each sack, with the oldest he began.
After searching all other sacks, the cup was found with Benjamin.

The men tore their clothes, and got back on their donkeys.
Now, they had to return to Joseph's house, in the city.
 Judah and his brothers, came to Joseph's house, in town.
When they saw him there, they fell before him, on the ground.

 Joseph said," What is this you've done, didn't you think I'd know?"
Judah said, "What can we say, O, can we clear our names?
 We are your servants, for the sin of your servants, God has found,
Both we, and he also, with whom the cup was found.

 Joseph said, "God forbid, that I should do such as that."
"But, the man in whom the cup is found, he is my servant!"
 "And as for the rest of you, get up in peace, to you father's house."
Then Judah came near to Joseph, and said, "My lord, oh."

 "Let me your servant, I pray, speak in my lord's ear,"
"For you are as Pharoah, so don't burn against me, your anger;"
 "But, you asked us, if we had a father or a brother, my lord."
"This is the child, of his old age, for our father is old!

 "His brother is dead, and he alone is left of his mother, and brother."
"His father loves him, and you asked us, to bring him, to you."
 "We told you, my lord, the lad can't leave his father, for this is why!
"If he should leave his father, his father would die."

 "You said, unless, our youngest brother, comes down with us,
"We could not see your face." "So then we told our father your words."
 "Our father said, "Go buy again!" And we said, "We can't go!"
"Without Benjamin, we can't see the man's face, no!"

 Judah said, "My father, your servant," said unto us, "You know my wife bare me 2 sons."
"One went out, and I've not seen him since."
 "I said surely, he is torn in pieces, and if you take this one, and mischief come,"
"You'll bring down, my gray hairs to the grave, with sorrow."

Joseph couldn't hid his feelings, from those that stood with him.
He cried, "Everyone, out from me!" Then no Egyptian stood with him.
   Then Joseph told his brothers, who he was, and Joseph wept out loud.
The Egyptians and Pharoah, heard him cry, aloud.

   Joseph said to his brothers, "I am Joseph, is my father alive?"
But they could not answer him, being troubled, by seeing him, alive.
   Then Joseph said, "Come near to me, I pray you."
Then all of them, came near to him there, too.

   Then Joseph said," I am Joseph your brother, who you sold, into Egypt."
"But don't be grieved or angry with yourselves, that you sold me, into Egypt."
   "For God, did send me here before you, to preserve your life."
"For, these last 2 years, there's been famine, and there's still five."

   "There are yet, five more year's famine, coming on the earth,"
"In which they'll be no earing or harvest."
   "So God sent me here, to preserve you and your posterity, on the earth."
"To save your lives, by a great deliverance."

   "So now, it was not you, that sent me here, but God."
"And God, made me a father, to Pharoah."
   "A lord also, and a ruler, over all his house."
"And in all the land of Egypt, throughout, for Pharoah."

   "So go quickly, to my father and say, your son Joseph, is alive!"
"And God hath made me lord of all Egypt, come down and see me!"
   "All your children, and children's children, herds and flocks."
"They will dwell, in the land of Goshen, and be near me, with all you've got."

   "There, will I nourish you, for there are yet, five years of famine.
"Lest, you and your families, and all you have, come to poverty, then."
   "All you've seen, all my glory in Egypt, go and tell my father."
"You shall hurry, and bring down to me, here, my father."

Joseph said, "Your eyes see me, and the eyes of my brother, Benjamin,"
"That it is, my mouth, that speaks to you men".
And Joseph fell, on his brother's neck and wept.
And Benjamin wept, on Joseph's neck."

Then Joseph kissed all his brothers, and wept on them.
And after that, his brothers talked to him;
The fame thereof was heard in Pharoah's house, saying "tell".
"Joseph's brothers are come," and it pleased Pharoah and his servants well.

And Pharoah said to Joseph, "Say to your brothers, this."
"Load up your donkey's and go, get yourselves, to Canaan Land."
"Get your father and households, and come to me."
"You'll see, the best of the Egypt, and have the best, of Egypt's land."

Pharoah, also commanded Joseph saying, "Have your brothers take wagons,"
"Let them take wagons, for their little ones and wives, out of the land of Egypt."
Pharoah said, "Bring your father and come, and don't care about your stuff."
"For the good, of all the land of Egypt is yours, and it's enough."

And Joseph gave them, wagons, as Pharoah had commanded him.
He gave to them provisions, for the way, and to all, changes of clothing.
But to Benjamin, Joseph gave 300 pieces of silver, and 5 changes of clothing.
To his father, he sent 10 donkeys, and from out of Egypt, good things.

Joseph sent, 10 she donkeys with bags of corn, bread and meat, for the way.
Joseph said, "See that you go, straight there," And sent his brother's away;
They came into the land of Canaan, unto Jacob, called Israel their father.
They told him, "Joseph is still alive and he over all Egypt, is governor."

And Jacob's heart fainted, for he did not believe, until he saw the wagons,
Which Joseph had sent, to carry him in. Then the spirit of their father, revived, again.
They told him, all the words of Joseph. And Israel said," Joseph is alive."
"It is enough," Jacob said, "I will go and see my son, before I die."

And Israel took his journey, with all that he had.
And when, coming to Beersheba,
    Israel offered, to the Lord God of heaven, sacrifices,
Unto the God, of his father, Isaac.

    And God spoke unto Israel, in the visions, of the night,
And said," Jacob, Jacob," and he said, "Here am I"
    And he said, "I am God, the God of thy father."
"Fear not to go down into Egypt."

    And God said," I will, go down with you, into Egypt.
And I will there, make of you, a great nation,
    "I will, surely, bring you up here, again!
And Joseph, shall put his hands, upon your eyes."

    And Jacob rose up, from Beersheba,
And carried their wives, and little one's;
    The sons of Israel, carried Jacob their father
For Pharoah, had sent them, to carry him and the family, in the wagons.

    And they took their cattle and their goods,
Which they had gotten, in the land of Canaan.
    Jacob and all his blood relatives with him.
Into Egypt's land, did come.

    All the souls, that came with Jacob, into Egypt's,
Which came out of his loins,
    All the souls were, sixty six persons, alive,
Not counting, Jacob's son's, wives.

And Israel, sent Judah, before himself, unto Joseph,
To direct his way, to Goshen.
And they came, into the land of Goshen.
And Joseph made ready his chariot, then.

And Joseph went up, to meet Jacob, his father.
To Goshen, came Joseph and presented himself, to him.
And Joseph fell, on his father's neck,
And Joseph wept, a good while, on his father's neck.

And Israel said unto Joseph,
"Now let me die.
Since I have seen your face,
Because, you are yet alive."

And Joseph said, to his father and brother's,
"I will go up and say, to Pharoah,
My father's house and brother's,
Which were in Canaan's land, are come to me."

"And the men, are shepherds,
And their trade, has been to feed cattle,
And they have brought, their flocks and herds,
And all, that they have.

Then Joseph said, "Whcn Pharoah calls you,
And ask you, what is your occupation?"
"Ye shall say, your servant's trade, hath been with cattle,
From our youth, even until now.'

"And our father, and grandfather's, also.
That you may dwell in Goshen's land."
"For, every shepherd, is an abomination,
Unto the Egyptians."

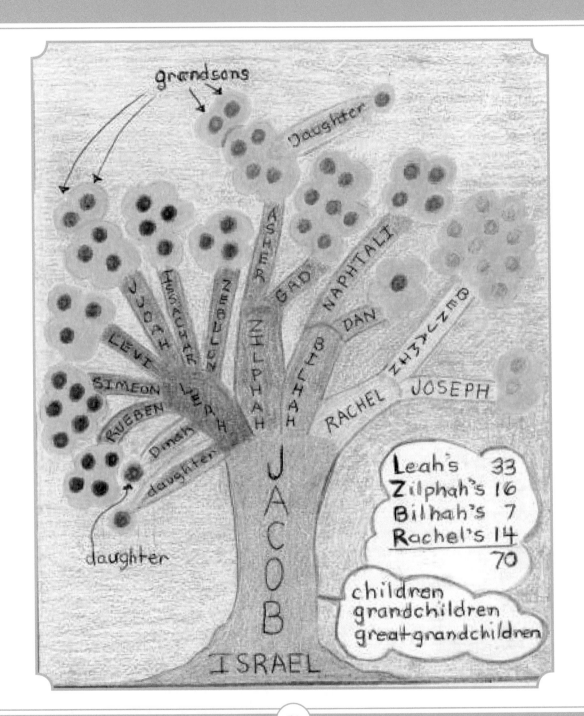

Now all the souls,s that came with Israel,
Out of Canaan's land,
Of the whole house of Jacob, were these.
His children, his grandchildren, and his great grandchildren.

Jacob's 1st son, Rueben and his 4 son's
Jacob's 2nd son, Simeon and his 6 son's
Jacob's 3rd son, Levi and his 3 son's,
Jacob's 4th son, Judah and his 3 son's, and 2 grandson's
Jacob's 5th son, Dan and his 1 son
Jacob's 6th son, Naphtali and his 4 son's
Jacob's 7th son, Gad and his 7 son's
Jacob's 8th son, Asher and his 4 son's, 1 daughter, and, 2 grandson's
Jacob's 9th son, Issachar and his 4 son's,
Jacob's 10th son, Zebulon, and his 3 son's
Jacob's 11th son, Benjamin and his 11 son's
Jacob's 2 daughter's Dinah and one unnamed. Gen. 37: 35, 45:15

Jacob came with 11 sons, 2 daughters, 49 grandsons,
1 granddaughter, 4 great granddaughter's, 66 in all;
Not counting their wives, Jacob coming too made, 67 in all.
But, counting Joseph and his 2 son's, there were 70, in all.

Now, Rachel had 2 sons for Jacob, Joseph and Benjamin.
Potipherah, the priest of On's daughter, Asenath,
Had 2 sons for Joseph, who were, Manasseh and Ephraim.
Born before the years of famine began. Gen. 41: 50

Jacob's 11th son was Joseph, and Joseph's 2 sons made 70,
Of Jacob's seed in Egypt, not counting wives, you see..
But, counting Jacob there were 71, descendants of Abraham,
And Isaac, in all to live in Canaans land.

Printed in the United States
By Bookmasters